My Power in Poetry

by
Gillian Flanders

My Power in Poetry

Copyright © 2020: Gillian Flanders

All rights reserved. No part of this publication may be produced, distributed, or transmitted in any form or by any means, including photocopying, recording, or other electronic or mechanical methods, without the prior written permission of the publisher, except in the case of brief quotations embodied in critical reviews and certain other non-commercial uses permitted by copyright law.

First Printed in United Kingdom 2020

Published by Conscious Dreams Publishing
www.consciousdreamspublishing.com

Edited by Elise Abram

Typeset by Oksana Kosovan

ISBN: 978-1-913674-37-3

Dedication

This book is dedicated to Elizabeth Ann Grant, my tin foot, the family matriarch. To all who read this book, big up u batty cos you know it's fatty

Foreword

My aunty was born in the swinging sixties. As I was growing up, she was the life and soul of every room, bus, park, or party she entered. She was like a cartoon character come to life, and you were sure to laugh until you cried when you were around her. I was always fascinated by her handwriting, and my grandmother always used to get her to write out all of her greeting cards. I would sit and watch her penmanship, mesmerised by how she wrote in such beautiful calligraphy so effortlessly. Her writing was art to me. Her outfits were art to me. She was art personified.

I know I am speaking as though my aunty has passed away, but she hasn't – she is alive and kicking and still cracking us all up; however, her lifestyle is considerably different now. As I became a teenager, my aunty had a breakdown due to a serious childhood trauma that had resurfaced and was affecting her mental health. We were all devastated by the news and rallied around her to support her in the best way we could. My aunty had always written poetry, but during this tumultuous time of downward spiralling and healing and repeating this cycle, she found her poetry to be a tool to help her through her difficult times. We loved it when she would share some of it with us, and we would all stare at her in awe of her beautiful handwriting. Everyone she ever met always said she had such a way with words and should be a writer. She agreed, and it was always something she aspired to do.

As well as suffering from issues around her mental health, she also had sickle cell anaemia, which hospitalised her when she was suffering badly. Then she was diagnosed with multiple sclerosis, and over time, her health has deteriorated. She is now unable to walk or take care of herself, and of course, we have all rallied around to support her again.

It was after a discussion with the family and a friend about my daughter's desire to write a book that we had the idea to publish some of my aunt's poetry to help fulfil her wish to become an author and show her that although she is physically incapable of a lot, it does not mean that life is over; far from it. This book has been created as evidence that you can start a new chapter of your life at any time, and that sometimes the worst situations can bear the fruits of your biggest blessings.

My aunty is one of the biggest blessings in my life, and we are creating this book in an attempt to bring her as much joy as she has brought me over the years, and because, maybe, her story or some of her poetry may do the same for someone else. This book and any others she may create will be her legacy. I love my aunty so much, and I truly hope you find a poem that you can love in this book.

All my love,
Forever your Nicky,
Tanty Scranty Gee
Gwangapapagungaya
XOXO

Contents

A Time To Be Silent 8
Birthday Surprise 10
Black And British 11
Book-Worms And Book-Knights 13
Concealed Beauty 15
Deejay Joe Grine 16
Equality 17
Fake And Nothing But 19
Happy Birthday, Retisha 20
Just To Spite The D.J 22
Division Belongs To Math "Not People" 23
Let's Honour-Our-Spirits 25
Live-Session: With My Wooley 26
Mourning Mass Feelings From The Heart 28
Mugs For Drugs 30
Offside 32
Poppi An Buggy Dem A Rave 33
Put Down The Gun 35
Rude Boy 36
The Magnificence Of A Good Man 37
Toxic-Love 39
You 40

About the Author 41
Acknowledgments 43

A Time To Be Silent

She's so happy. Don't tell her! Please, don't breathe a word
It doesn't make sense to repeat what you've heard
Some people spread rumours, but know they are lies
So never believe, till you've seen with your eyes
So what if you heard from a reliable source
The tongue often lies with a powerful force
Causing the pain of a knife or a sword
Wounding so many and sowing discord
If you want my opinion? I think it's a lie
Spread not this bad rumour, and soon it will die
She need not hear gossip from you or from me
Or anyone blind to the truth they can't see
I'm not gonna tell her. I give you my word
Her husband's NOT sleeping-around, THAT'S ABSURD!
He's honest and faithful. I give him my trust
So good to his wife and the kids. EVEN US!
But if it IS true that he's sleeping-around,
She may think of the KIDS, not divorce on those grounds
He's innocent till proven he's guilty of this
If it's TRUE, she'll find out, but then ignorance is bliss
It could be that she knows, but is willing to strive
She has true inner-strength and she'd fight to survive

She's so happy, I tell you. So happy in life
And she STILL can't believe that he made her his wife
But the point that I'm making to you, DON'T YOU SEE?
Is never cause sadness or disharmony
'Cos life is too short and sometimes it gets rough
We ALL have to struggle with troubles and stuff
It's a real heavy load when disasters occur
But out-weighing-them-all is a vicious rumour

(*1997*)

Birthday Surprise

This poem is dedicated to all loving, caring, and 'faithful' men

A Black couple I know had a baby one-night,
but no-one predicted that he would be white
No, I'm not being silly! Believe me, it's true
His hair is so golden. His eyes are light, too
When the parents first saw him, they said the surprise
made them feel like they couldn't believe their own eyes
Biologically theirs. It's a matter of fact
But ignorant questions still have an impact
The-Black-mother-conceived of the Black father's sperm
And many-a-test can be made to confirm
It's a common occurrence. It's not even rare
But still many people aren't even aware
And jokers are having the time of their life
Saying, "When will the milkman stop bonking your wife?"
A birth is so special. So how can they joke?
Do they realise the anger and pain they provoke?
People say they've adopted. But what do they know?
'Cos 'the system' quite often won't let this be so
Blacks-raising-white-children to them is not right
but people are equal. Black, yellow, brown, and white
The mother confessed there was no instant bond
But after a while, she grew more than just fond
He is loved just as much as their other Black son
What a beautiful way Black and white become one

(*1996*)

Black And British

I'm Black, and I'm British My chosen description
I haven't been branded; it's not an inscription
I feel very British. And I'm right to say,
My people back home would see me in this way
Where my parents were born is my spiritual home
My roots and my blood and the core of my bone
But I call myself British; it's nothing deceitful
It doesn't mean I'd turn my back on my people
I was born over here, and I'm okay with that
It isn't a sin to be British and Black
But I'm still a person who's not very able
to deal with society's need for these labels
'Cos some blacks in Britain are getting confused,
Undecided on which silly label to choose
Some say they're West Indian not British at all
'Cos the racism here makes them feel so appalled
But be honest – if you took a short break in Spain,
If assumed to be British, I doubt you'd complain
In fact, you're more likely to quickly agree
Without even thinking, quite naturally
Though you're proud to deny you are British when here,
During holiday-time, you admit loud and clear
For the strength of an accent so often reveals
Our country of birth, minus birthplace ideals
See, if one day in Britain out shopping you went,
You met a Black man, and his accent was French,
You would say he was French when describing the man

But he might see himself as a true-African
Your identity's simply how you see yourself
But respect disagreement from anyone else
Because though you may find the description for you,
Understand many others won't see that way, too
So many have hate for the country they're born
But let's make ourselves part of it. Weather the storm
For Black can be British, American, and French
Does the home in your heart really feel so intense?
Make a choice. Keep in mind the majority's view
Decide for or against, or don't even pursue

(1996)

Book-Worms And Book-Knights

My favourite table's booked, but I'm SO late
I find a man there, reading as he ate
He's broad and smartly dressed, but unaware
Of my attention while I'm standing there
His head's bent down, engrossed in his book
Please, raise it now, and show me how you look
So much for books; the man just read my mind
And I can see he's quite a handsome find
He smiles at me, and he closely observes
Whilst physical attraction wrecks my nerves
This must be what they call 'love at first sight '
'Cos, gosh, I'm feeling something here tonight
I hope I get to talk to him somehow
Not yet – the waiter's coming over now

WAITER:
Madam is late We thought you wouldn't show,
and I'm afraid we've let your table go.
You're free to choose another, so please do.
I'll bring Madame the a-la-carte menu.

LADY:
With hesitance, I find myself a seat,
behind this handsome man was too discreet.
Oh, what a bad decision I've just made.
He must think a snub has been displayed.

HANDSOME MAN:
Excuse me, please, but I just overheard,
your conversation clearly, every word.
We're both aware my table's really yours.

When no-one came, I took it with just cause.
But now I MUST INSIST on swapping seats
　　As you intended sitting here to eat.

LADY:
That's kind. I don't mind swapping if you don't.
　　I feel you'll be persistent if I won't.
　　　　You cunning man
You've swapped YOUR CHAIR with mine
While keeping THE SAME TABLE all the time.

HANDSOME MAN:
I never mentioned swapping tables though,
　　But I feel really guilty now you know.
　　Forgive me for the rotten trick I played,
But now you're here I'd love it if you stayed.

LADY:
To share with you is not against my will.
But just to make things clear, I'LL PAY MY BILL.
　　Oh, by the way, please can I take a look
　　Before you seemed so lost inside your book.

HANDSOME MAN:
Yes.
And I've finished, keep it if you want.
It's called 'Love at First Sight in Restaurant'.
One look at you has made me feel the same,
So let me buy the finest house Champagne

(1996)

Concealed Beauty

Tonight is the night when I meet my 'BLIND DATE!'
I'm dying to 'SEE HIM'. I really can't wait!
We've talked on the phone. 'CONVERSATION JUST FLOWS'
I feel like he's someone I already know
I'll put on the black dress?? Or maybe the red??
'NO!' that dress says, 'Baby, please take me to bed!'
At long last, I'm ready, but so full of nerves
'Cos this man is 'SPECIAL. ' He's 'just what I deserve'
I'm here at the restaurant and he chose the place
'IT'S LOVELY!' Hope I say the same for 'HIS FACE'.
I dreamt he'd be 'drop-dead ' but now I can see
'HE LOOKS LIKE HE'LL DROP DEAD FROM LOOK-BAD DISEASE.'
This can't be the guy! It just can't! 'OH, PLEASE GOD!'
I'm sorry to say 'HE'S A RIGHT UGLY DOG!'
I can't bear to kiss him. I'll just turn my cheek
But he kisses my 'HAND', and then helps with my seat
I start to feel guilty for judging by looks
Bad-covers can hide the contents of good-books
So, we talk, and we laugh, and we laugh, and we talk
Then we finish the date with a slow moonlit walk
That was five years ago, but the memory will stay
'"COS WE'RE MARRIED, AND CHILD NUMBER THREE'S ON THE WAY "

(1997)

Deejay Joe Grine

AY AY ………YO ……RAAAH ………'JOE GRINE??'
A-U-DAT??………SKIDIPA-A-CAAHL-U
YEHS MISSA BAAHS-MUHN, ME CUM AGEN EAZI NA
IZ WOT KINE-A CHEEKEE NAYME U 'AVE DEH DREAD??
LAAAHRD! 'ME WELL LARFIN '
ME WAN BEG U ANUDDA SHOUWT-OUWT PLEEZE !
TEHL DA LISSENA DEM 'WOOLEY AN SKIDIPA BESS
FREN FAH LYFE!'
TANK-U-BAAHS
U WELL TAAHT ME DIDDA LEEVE U EHNIT??…………
COULDDA NEHVA
ME WELL FAAHL FAH U DAAHLIN. 'ME REELY MASHIN-
UP NOW '
WON LOV EHVRY TYME MISSA DEEJAY PAYSH X X X.

(*1996*)

Equality

'Women, don't fool yourselves. It's not okay to sleep-around
Yes, I know men cheat. It hurts
But you need not lower your moral standards in retaliation
Stop living by lust and anger. It controls you, can't you see that?
What have you become? Look at you! What have you become?
Your 'search' for 'Mr Right' has become a 'hunt' for 'Mr One-night'
And your arrow still carries the blood of your last victim
Constantly, you plan how to snare the next unsuspecting man you desire
Then devour him whole and 'spit him out'
Your purpose fulfilled. Your need satisfied. You make ready your weapon…
As you hasten to make your next swift killing
The equality you say you want with men has stripped you of your femininity
You are loud and forward and detest domesticity
Your presence is not known at your house. You're never at home
Who can reach you there? Tell me, who?
The words from your mouth show no modesty or decency
They are not befitting, even for a man
You discuss your many conquests, leaving nothing to the imagination
Blinded to the fact you discredit yourself more than that of your subject
You call yourself assertive, but you fail to see you are just aggressive
And in your folly, you ridicule any man gracious enough to show women chivalry

It's yourself and womankind you put to shame
Your denial is weak, but your self-righteousness strengthens your ignorance
Repeatedly, you refuse instruction
You are your own leader
And with speed, you guide yourself to inevitable destruction

(1996)

Fake And Nothing But

And so, his love was not real…and now, fake love has gone
He's finished playing with my heart and stringing me along
I was just someone that was there, suspecting not his ploy
No doubt he's found some other fool whose heart he can destroy

(*1997*)

Happy Birthday, Retisha

Throughout our lives, we women
have to face some tough decisions,
but once our minds are made-up,
we proceed to gain our vision.

I've asked for God to bless
your surgeon's hands with vital skill,
so when you come around,
you'll know that he's achieved your will.

Your wisdom has revealed to you
there is no loss or gain,
for soon you'll be forever free
from all that constant pain.

So concerned
about your health,
The plans you have around your home
will make time quickly pass.
Then, all your friends at work will say,
"Retisha's back at last"

Embrace each lovely moment
that your future holds in store.
God's blessings will astound you
like you've never seen before.

The last time that we spoke, you said,
"I'll reach my ideal weight."
I'm sure you're fine.
I pray to God, you'll meet an ideal date.

I know you've bought some great new clothes,
so dump your fashion fades
and 'strut your stuff' so all can see
'AT 40 YOU'RE A BABE '

Just To Spite The D.J.

...and that was a brilliant track off the album,
up three places to number eight this week.
You're listening to London's hottest number-one station...
don't touch that di...ssschhh...warm and dry...ssschh...climbing high...
ssschhh...your requests...ssschhh...special guest...
ssschhh...concert in June...ssschhh...WICKED TUNE
...ssschhh...on the line...ssschhh...down to nine...
ssschhh...favourite station...ssschhh...dedications...
ssschhh...and you can catch him again tomorrow, same time.
You're listening to London's hottest number-one station,
don't touch that di...ssschhh.

Division Belongs To Math "Not People"

GIRLFRIEND:
MANY THINK OUR LOVE IS WRONG
And opinions have been strong
When WE'RE WALKING HAND-IN-HAND along the street.
But once I pulled away my hand,
Turned, and said, 'Please, understand
THAT'S MY MUM right there and YOU Two MUSTN'T MEET '

BOYFRIEND:
Babe, you should've said before
Don't keep SECRETS anymore
Are you scared SHE WON'T ACCEPT WE'RE GOING OUT?
Look, I'll go before she comes
We'll talk later, at MY MUM'S
But listen YOU'RE THE ONE I COULDN'T LIVE WITHOUT

GIRLFRIEND'S MUM:
You were talking to that guy
Who is he? And don't you lie!
What the heck is going on? I want the truth
Forget it. I'm not BLIND, you know
YOU WERE HOLDING HANDS NOW GO
Get back home AND PACK YOUR BAGS. I've got my PROOF

GIRLFRIEND:
Oh, look, Mum – HE'S JUST A FRIEND

GIRLFRIEND'S MUM:
No, he isn't. Don't pretend
You've been seeing him behind my bloody back

GIRLFRIEND:
Yes, I have and now you know,
I will gladly pack and go
YOU'RE A RACIST and YOU HATE HIM 'COS HE'S BLACK

GIRLFRIEND'S MUM:
So? I've got two black son-in-laws
Who, you know, I JUST ABHOR
You're no better than YOUR SISTERS are, I see

GIRLFRIEND:
Prepare for THREE BLACK SON-IN-LAWS
And NO DAUGHTERS ANYMORE
'Cos YOU'VE CUT-THEM-OFF and NOW YOU'RE LOSING ME

Let's Honour-Our-Spirits

So much is divided between 'GOOD' and 'BAD'.
And choosing the 'GOOD' makes our spirits so glad
We honour our 'FIVE-SENSES' in the 'RIGHT-WAY'
'LET'S HONOUR OUR SPIRITS DON'T LET THEM DECAY
We can 'TOUCH' something 'BAD' like a slimy wet slug
We can 'TOUCH' something 'GOOD' like a soft Persian-Rug
We can 'TASTE' something 'BAD' like a stale piece of bread
We can 'TASTE' something 'GOOD' like a cherry so red
We can 'HEAR' something 'BAD' like a car on the street's alarm
We can 'HEAR' something 'GOOD' like soft music that's calm
We can 'SEE' something 'BAD' like a bloody, dripping nose
We can 'SEE' something 'GOOD' like a sun that has just rose
We can 'SMELL' something 'BAD' like the rotting of meat
We can 'SMELL' something 'GOOD' like a perfume, so sweet
In all that I've mentioned, I bet you'd choose 'GOOD'
The 'BAD' we reject, I'm sure everyone would
But we get into fussing. We get into fights
And damage our spirits – it just isn't right
Let's think 'POSITIVE' and follow it through
'Cos positive's 'GOOD', it's the right-thing-to-do

(June 2013)

Live-Session: With My Wooley

For my devoted littal-daahlin – Mr Wooley Tyson

Yoo 'singh' fore a 'greyt-banned ' caahl 'Misty-in-Roots'
Yore populah 'whurl-wyde' widd 'addults an yoots'

Yoo aahsked if eye wanted to 'heer-da-banned-play'
An sedd eye shood 'Cum-ouwt-da-'ouwse ' fore da day

Eye-alwayz-hadd-wanted-to 'heer-"YOO"-pIay-live'
An-eye-couldnt-wayt fore da coach to arrive

Da journee woz lohng An-wee-went-aahl-arouwn
Wee drove on da coach till da venue woz fouwn

Wee-sat-drinkin-wine-until 'tyme-fore-yore-caahll'
'An sew menny peeple filled-uhp-da-daahnce-haahll'

Sum-guy-sedd-to-mee, 'Eye 'ave 'erd dem beefor
Eye cant 'elp meeself! Eye-jus-cum-bak-fore-mor'

Eye wanted to say 'Da-lead-singher's-my-frehn'
buht-I-woodn't-'ave-'fit-in' widd-aahl-da-crouwd-dehn

At-won-poynt-wee-sore 'aahl-da-lites-dissapeer'
buht jus lyke a 'pro,' 'yoo-sang-on-widdout-feer'

'Da vybe woz sew good!' Wee-AAHL-'Couldn't-Stohp-Daahnce'
'Eye-broc-ouwt-a-wine-lyke-it-woz-my-laahs-chaahnce'

Eye jus fellt SEW VEX wen da nite hadd to ehn
Eye wanted to heer yoo 'agen an agen'

Da peeple wer clappin an cheerin yoo, too
'Eye-hadd-sew-much-fun-dat-woz-WEHLL-OVADUE'

'Oh, Wooley Dat nite eye will nehva- forgeht
Eye-think-ov-it- "NOW" widdout-ehny-regreht '

(*Wednesday, 7 August 2013*)

Mourning Mass Feelings From The Heart

I camped out on the street one night but found it hard to sleep
Because the death of Princess Di kept my thoughts so deep
Her works of good outshine the bad, for even when in plight
our princess didn't weaken as she fought for what was right
So many strangers round me but one purpose for us all
and that is to be present at Diana's funeral
I lit a candle in her name and read beside its glow
the scriptures from my Bible to prepare for tomorrow
For that will be the time to say, 'Goodbye, dear friend, God bless'
You're the Queen of Many Hearts, the true People's Princess
Then morning came, and I arose with such a sense of peace
I stood and watched the massive crowds, continually increase
There seemed to be a bonding-force, of this I was aware
so I joined a group of people; I'm so glad they were there
They helped me climb the barriers to get a better view
of the road on which the cortege and the coffin would pass through
They cheered me up so much I found it possible to laugh
but many tears were cried when the procession took the path
United in our mourning, sharing comfort in our grief
until the worst was over, and we only felt relief
The time had finally come for us to-go-our-separate-ways
but we exchanged our numbers, so in contact, we could stay
I felt an overwhelming need to keep in touch with Frank
Our meeting was a blessing, and I've only God to thank
So, I gave a hug to Danny, and a goodbye hug to Jo
but more of an embrace to Frank – it hurt to let him go

The way I felt surprised me (after all, we'd barely met)
but since that very day, on him, my mind is truly set
That day was full of meaning, and I learned some valid things
Most of all, to be more caring, 'cos who knows what life may bring?
The Princess's life has ended, so it's time for us to start
taking interest in the needy, like Diana, Queen of Hearts.

Mugs For Drugs

Mack and Jack are taking CRACK –
they used to study hard, but now they're both so slack
They once were bright, and my delight
was to study with them, even on a party night
Jane, Shane, Wayne, and Lorraine
spent their fees for university on damn COCAINE –
I felt so stunned, and everyone
Couldn't believe they were pulling out
because they wanted more fun
Steve and Scott do WEED and POT –
it's taken their ambition, so that's all they've got
They've had so much that they've lost touch
I reckon even now the drugs are in their clutch
Jim and Marilyn adore HEROINE –
they always fail to hand assignments in
They've helped me twice with good advice,
but they don't give or take it, now that they're hooked on vice
Danny and Chris are on CANNABIS –
the year before their habit, they had Grade-A-bliss
They worked their brains, in class they reigned
but now their minds are bordering on sheer derange
Denise and Louise refuse to believe
they're risking their lives whenever taking E's
They'd planned to teach, but now they preach
how safe they think the drug is 'cos they take two each
And then there's me, but I'm DRUG-FREE –
the only thing I ever crave is my Degree

But all the rest have lost interest
and any mention of it makes them so depressed
They seem so close to comatose
I'm really scared that one of them will overdose
I often cry and scream-out WHY?
I wish they'd give-it-up, but they won't even TRY
Their parents' tears reveal the fear
of living with the worry that the end is near
So, addicts, learn through self-concern
YOU'VE GOT TO STOP IT NOW,
AND NEVER DARE RETURN

(1996)

Offside

WIFE: You've hidden the remote
HUSBAND: No, I haven't! You're mad
W: Look – the film's gonna start
H: So is football, too bad
W: You said you'd give football a miss for the day
H: Well, you know I'm a liar – why trust what I say?
W: You make me so sick – did you hear what I said?
H: Yeah, my words exactly – OH-COME-ON-YOU-RE-EDS
W: Turn-it-down. It's too loud! Gosh, the neighbours can hear!
H: Look – enough of your nagging. Go get me a beer
W: Go get it yourself! What d'ya think that I am?
And why can't you pick-up those empty beer cans?
H: For goodness' sake, SHUT-IT! I'm not in the mood
You clean up the mess and get me some food
W: Does m'Lord want more fags? There is only one left
Or would Sir prefer to be beaten to death?
H: Haha, very funny! Now, go and GET LOST!
I'm Ref of this row, and you've just been sent-off!

Poppi An Buggy Dem A Rave

We dun jinkin Whiskee an Rum in da pub
Soh-me-an-me-Possee-dem-gan-to-da-club

Oh laahrd, chek da bredda deh, bussin a skank
An look pon 'im woornan she-fayva-well-rank

Ay Buggy Chek Gupta an Gungadin, too
Dem cum wid da hole addee Turbin-Edd Crew

Cum dance wid me Buggy! An-hug-me-up-good
Before Fiyaah-Gun an dem start fee lik-wood

Pum-Pum. Wikid-Choon! Big-Up-My-Selekta!
"We goh cum ear agen ca it good na Rasta "

Ay Marcia cum Lehwee do Dutty-Wine
jus-squeez-me-up-Buggy. An grab my behine

Look dat pregnant one wid she belly well big
she gan 'ave it now Dread ta Bombo-Rahtid

Ay Buggy, dat man beg-a-dance-wid-Michelle
But she tell 'im 'Raaairh -Butters-Bwoy Goh-bak-to-'ell '

Raaaah! Look pon dat, Sue! She nah weirin na close
An all dat she wan fee do, stan-up-an-pose

Whaaaht? Joe pynch 'er batty! But chek 'ow she smyle
She-tink-she-well-nyce, but she nah 'ave na style

Dat-bredda deh-Joe nose dat Sue iz well-loose
But wach 'im na, Nicky. 'im fayva mongoose

An chek a nex gyal, in she Batty-Rydaah
She lookin well junk widee-Fiyaah-Waahtah

Oh, Laahrd Gad, she drap! 'Ay-gyal-gyet-up-ya-betch
Aan covaah ya badi ya-dyam-nasti-retch!'

Laaaaahrd! Look wot she weirin! Gaaaaahd! Wot dee gyal tink?
She batty well hairee! An she coon-coon well stink!

'Yo Buss-a-nex-Rydim! Ay! Put-off-da-Lite!
Ca-me-an-me-Possee-dem-nah-leeve-tonite!'

Whaaaht? Look-pon-da- tyme, Chars! It gan six ocloc
We cyant get nah taxi beeca-da-road-bloc

'Da playc it well mash-up! Wid-lik-wood-an-gun'
but 'tek me nex week, Buggy! Man, add fun!

(2013)

Put Down The Gun

Where are the LOVE AND PEACE under the sun??
I just want my people to PUT DOWN THE GUN
THEY'RE CARRYING KNIVES, and THEY'RE JOINING GANGS, too
They act like there's nothing else for them to do
THEY LOVE ONLY MONEY AND DONT VALUE LIFE
To them, it's such fun when they cause someone strife
STABBING AND SHOOTING, dealing-DRUGS ON THE STREET
And that's what they think makes their life so complete
PRAISING THE EVIL and HURTING THE GOOD
And SPREADING SUCH FEAR through the whole neighbourhood
They think of the gang as blood-brothers or kin
But too many times there is trouble within
Sometimes they WISE-UP and they just WANT TO LEAVE
But fear makes it too hard for them to proceed
I say, 'GET-OUT RUN-AWAY DONT-LOOK-BACK
THIS LIFE IS DESTROYING YOU So is the crack
Stop stabbing and shooting and dealing-the-drugs
THE GANG ARE YOUR ENEMIES, and they're all thugs '
So, PUT DOWN THE GUN, and YOUR TROUBLES WILL CEASE
And I know a way you can find LOVE AND PEACE
TURN YOUR LOVE FOR THE GANG INTO LOVE FOR OUR-LORD
God's love, in return, has THE GREATER REWARD
START READING THE BIBLE, and soon you will see
That truly THE BEST THINGS IN LIFE ARE ALL FREE

(2013)

Rude Boy

So, you're rougher than rough. You're tougher than tough
The words from your mouth contain nothing but cuss
You're frontin', you're tough. Your crime you discuss
Your manners are equal to pigs in a trough
You drip in gold lush with diamonds encrust
And show no remorse towards stealing the stuff
Your car is so plush, there's gold in your cuff
But your greed equals nothing is ever enough
You show no concern for the poor living rough
And think they deserve to eat nothing but 'brough'
You're smugly so chuffed, you've gained someone's trust
But later, with sorrow, they'll realise your bluff
You smoke-out your stuff, then kick-up a fuss
'Cos someone has trod on your shoe in a crush
The going gets tough. You're losing your puff
Police catch you up and snap on the handcuff
So, you're rougher than rough?? You're tougher than tough??
Wake-up Smell-the-coffee
ENOUGH IS ENOUGH

(*1996*)

The Magnificence Of A Good Man

This poem is dedicated to all loving, faithful, spiritual men.

Thou art wondrous, my love. Thou art darker than the deepest mahogany
and thy muscle as solid as iron
Thou art as mysterious as the foreign lands in which thy dwelleth
and the sound of thy laughter hath the wealth of nature's beauty
Oh, thou, my beloved, the height of the mountains overshadow you not
Neither doth the ferocity of wild beasts bring you fear
See how gentle doth my beloved's hands caress
and with great strength doth attend to workmanship
My love is magnificent for the eye to behold,
and thy teeth are the colour of pure snow
Thy precious head is adorned with glistening locks as black as rich onyx
and thy dark body as hard as diamonds
Thy mouth alone is glorified
Thy covereth thy words with the fine silk of intelligence,
and teacheth mouths of thorns to speaketh wholesome wisdom and righteousness
Thy tender loving-kindness is extended to all abundantly,
and all in receipt praiseth you so
My womb continually yearneth to be full
for thou loveth the produce thereof with great affection
and looketh well to my needs in the season I beareth
Our sons are fine young men who feareth God, possesseth great wisdom,
and reflecteth your many good qualities

Our daughters equalleth womankind in graceful perfection
and hath much virtue, honour, and chastity
Oh, my love. My love. My dearest beloved
You maketh my soul to scream with joy
You completeth my whole existence
'Tis thou who continually remindeth me and all to carrieth our
blackness with pride
Thou art great among the people of our lands, exceeding in honour
and righteousness
and hath much wisdom concerning the mysteries of the earth
Twilight forever gleams in my beloved's dark eyes
and there's none who can reflect his magnificence for the endurance
of all time

(*1996*)

Toxic-Love

I've just had my baby. I'm feeling so glad
But my boyfriend says that he's not the child's dad
I love him so much, and I never would cheat
But he says I'm selling myself on the street
I cry every night, and I beg him to say
that he loves me, too, and he believes me today.
He says I'm a liar. He says he wants proof
to show he's the father of my baby Ruth
So down at the hospital, they take a swab
of my little baby and my boyfriend, Bob.
The baby needs things he's refusing to give
even though the test showed a clear positive
He smokes too much "pot", and it causes conceit
He says I'm a prostitute working the street
And he keeps-on drinking too much alcohol
He just doesn't stop when he's out of control
He's cruel, and he doesn't show love for his child
And he's still accusing me of running wild
I've just had enough, so I'm going to pack
all of my belongings and never look back
I know I will struggle, and it will be hard,
but my love for my baby will keep me on guard.
I'll move far away, and I'll get a good job,
'cos there is no way that I'll go back to Bob
I'll better myself with much prayer to the Lord,
'cos I was a church-goer, then I got bored.
But I'm going back, and this time I will stay,
'cos now there is nothing to stand in my way.
More blessings upon us will come in good time.
Oh, me and my baby are gonna be fine

(*February 2013*)

You

Oh, my darling, you inspire me
You fuel desire's fire in me
You strengthen my weaknesses with your positivity
and relinquish my fears
My thoughts are your visibility. You reach into my mind
and caress your findings there. Past loves escape your grasp
They exist not in my thoughts by your tender destruction
You tell me that my words are healing. That you can taste my words
and digest them into your innermost being
I know you do. I taste yours, too
I remember clearly when we met, when I first tasted your words,
when loves were lost, and sadness had robbed me of inner-peace
A famine of love and understanding had set upon me
I spoke, but no one seemed to hear me I cried an ocean,
but sails were set for the voyage of goodbye
I had no one. I was so alone. So alone. So very, very alone
But you came to me
I looked into your eyes and suddenly
I felt a sense of peace
Like the comfort of a warm embrace had touched me,
and then, you fed me. You fed me happiness
Oh, my love, I tasted every word
You nourished me constantly
and prevented the bitter taste of sadness from choking me
I devoured your every word with savage hunger
and quenched my thirst with the champagne of your wisdom
You are my heart's joy. My life. My everything. My love for you is
endless. And I adore you

(1996)

About the Author

Gillian Flanders braves all four seasons in a day from her West London residence with visits three times a day from her fantastic care team that helps look after her along with the family. Before her health complications, she had a career using her dulcet-toned voice at some of London's biggest West End hotel switchboards, which she really enjoyed, alongside her poetry and freelance writing.

When she isn't writing, you might find Gillian watching her favourite cooking shows and game shows, and then instructing everyone about which new recipe she would like to try (try as in taste – we get sent to cook it, of course). Gillian has an insatiable love for music, and when she gets a favourite song into her head, it's not long before we all know the words.

This is Gillian's debut book, and we hope the first of many.

It is with great sadness that we have to announce that our beloved sister Gillian passed away on the 14th of January 2021, her book of poetry is her legacy left for all of us to enjoy. As a family we were able to present her with this book as a surprise Christmas present and the look on her face will be eternally etched in our hearts and we will never be able to fill the humongous void she has left so we say to her rest in peace, we love you so much, Run Dance your Free.

In loving memory to a beautiful daughter, wonderful sister, and special Aunty, a friend to many people, we salute you.

Acknowledgments

First and foremost, I thank God for giving me the ability to make this book possible.

I would like to thank my wonderful mother (Tinfoot) for her love and strength. Bringing up five of us was not easy, and boy were we loud and still are.

I also want to thank my sisters Retisha (Diva), Hazel (Shortfoot) and my brothers, Desmond (Diggo-D) and Lesley (Shortknee). He took so long to grow! What a rollercoaster of a ride. From the kid's homes in Brighton, then Basildon and finally our home in Southall. What a cultural melting pot! We had a lot of laughter, tears and the many ups and downs that come along with being in a big family. Then, as time went by, along came my nieces and nephew.

Charlotte (Chubby Cheeks) and her children Indiahna, Davontae and baby Shyloe also Courtney (Coco Bean) and their lovely mother Samantha (Red Hair). What a joy watching you all grow. But one niece in particular, Nicole (Nick Nicks) who, after much discussion with the family and her monumental help and drive, made the publishing of this book possible. She also has a daughter I adore, Miamie-Rae (Little Dolly Dumpling).

I want to thank everyone who has helped and supported me in my good and bad times.

My carers Deco, Noella and Amira.

A very special thanks to Steve (Stewie), who has been a power of strength and continues to help out whenever he can. You are all very much appreciated.

I can't forget my sweet, sweet, sweet Grenada. Also my special Uncle Ben and Aunty Olive and the many people I met on my island in the sun.

Last but not least, a very special thank you to everyone at Conscious Dreams Publishing and Daniella Blechner, (who true to her company's name, has consciously and graciously made my dream come true) for your patience and time spent on making this a reality.

I now have a book, *My Power in Poetry*! Gwangapapagungaya!! Thank you, God!!!

Conscious Dreams
PUBLISHING

Be the author of your own destiny

Find out about our authors, events, services and how you too can get your book journey started.

- Conscious Dreams Publishing
- @DreamsConscious
- @consciousdreamspublishing
- Daniella Blechner
- www.consciousdreamspublishing.com
- info@consciousdreamspublishing.com

Let's connect

www.ingramcontent.com/pod-product-compliance
Lightning Source LLC
Chambersburg PA
CBHW071548080526
44588CB00011B/1833